# Taming
# the Dragon

Written by Samantha Montgomerie

Illustrated by Evelline Andrya

## Collins

# Chapter 1

Red lanterns line the streets for miles. People come to see them shine.

It is time to see in the new year.

Ling ties up his apron. "Time to stack these plates," says Yin.

Ling spoons in the filling and folds the dumplings.
He lines them up on a tray.

The remaining dumplings go on the plates.
"Yay! Now it's time for the dragon," says Yin.

She twirls out of the kitchen. Ling frowns.

# Chapter 2

Ling gazes at the clock. Soon it will be time for the dragon.

"Maybe I can hide inside," thinks Ling.

Ling remembers his dream about the dragon's big jaws. He shudders in fear.

Smoke had snorted from its nose as it swiped its sharp claws.

The loud drum beats outside. "Time to go!" yells Yin.

Ling takes a big gulp of air. It's time to tame the dragon. "This dragon brings luck, not like the one in my dream," he reminds himself.

People line the sides of the street. Nan cranes her neck.

"Here it comes!" says Nan. The drum beat hammers inside Ling's chest.

The dragon snakes near Ling. Its scales flash and its jaws snap.

The dragon rises up in the air. Ling gulps.

# Chapter 3

Under the flash of the dragon's scales, Ling spots Yin. The dragon's tail swirls with her.

Yin winks at Ling. *This looks fun*, thinks Ling.

Golden sparks pop and shine, sprinkling like glitter across the black night.

"Make a new year's wish!" says Nan.

Ling gazes at the lanterns as they flutter and sway.
The moon shines behind them.

"Next year, I want to make the dragon swirl with Yin," wishes Ling.

# Chinese New Year

Chinese New Year starts on the first new moon.
It runs for 16 days.

Lanterns of all shapes and sizes hang in the streets.

People eat particular foods. They join parades.

dumplings

# Six Chinese New Year foods and what they bring

fish

good fortune

dumplings

riches

spring rolls

gold

persimmons

good fortune

wontons

riches

nuts

a long life

27

# How to make a paper lantern

1. Fold the paper.

2. Cut strips from the folded end.

### 3. Loop the paper to form a tube.

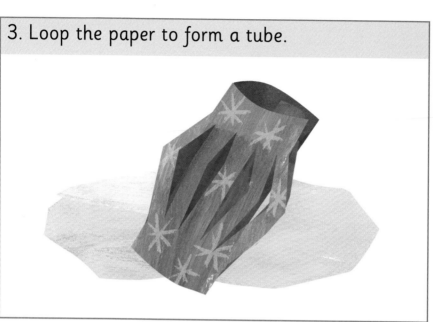

### 4. Tape up the ends.

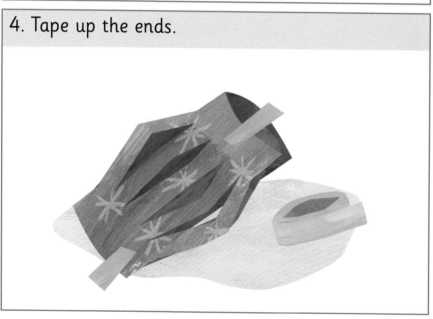

# Taming the dragon

# 🐾 Review: After reading 🐾

Use your assessment from hearing the children read to choose any GPCs, words or tricky words that need additional practice.

## Read 1: Decoding
- Reread the title and ask: What does **taming** mean? (e.g. *calming it down, making less wild*) Encourage the children to think further about the word **taming** by asking: Do you think the dragon at the celebration is tame or wild?
- Ask the children to find the following sounds on these pages. Ask: How are they spelt?
  p 4 /ee/ (**th<u>e</u>se**)   p 8 /ai/ (**g<u>a</u>z<u>e</u>s**)   p 12 /oa/ (**g<u>o</u>**)   p 9 /igh/ (**ins<u>i</u>d<u>e</u>**)
- Challenge the children to pick a page and read it aloud fluently, sounding any words they are uncertain of silently in their heads.
- Bonus content: Ask the children to search for a word that contains the /yoo/ sound on pages 26 and 27. (**fort<u>u</u>n<u>e</u>**)

## Read 2: Prosody
- Turn to pages 20 and 21, and discuss the atmospheric scene. Can the children find words on page 20 that bring the scene to life? (e.g. *pop, shine, glitter*)
- Ask the children to read page 20 aloud, making these words sound like the things they mean. For example say: Can you say **pop** like the sound? Can you emphasise the "t" in **glitter**?
- Encourage the children to read page 21. Point out how Nan's words might be said excitedly and loudly, over the noise of the fireworks.
- Bonus content: Can the children read pages 28 and 29, as if they were a television presenter, giving the audience clear instructions?

## Read 3: Comprehension
- Reread the title and ask: Have you seen or read any stories about dragons? Encourage the children to talk about dragons in different stories and cultures and think about their similarities and differences.
- Return to pages 14 and 15. Ask: What special event is being celebrated here? (*Chinese New Year*)
- Encourage the children to consider the importance of Ling's dream in the story. Ask: What was the dragon like in his dream? (e.g. *big jaws, sharp claws*)
  o Ask: Which words show how Ling felt about the dragon in his dream? (**shudders in fear**)
  o Turn to pages 16 and 17 and ask: Which words make this dragon sound similar to the dragon in the dream? (e.g. *jaws snap*)
  o Ask: Do you think the dream had a big effect on Ling? How? (e.g. *it made the new year dragon seem more scary than it really was*)
- Turn to pages 30 and 31 and ask the children to retell the story of Ling and the dragon in their own words, using the pictures as reminders.